Financial Services and the Single Currency

Robert Leach

Croner Publications Ltd
Croner House
London Road
Kingston upon Thames
Surrey KT2 6SR
Tel: 0181-547 3333

Published by
Croner Publications Ltd
Croner House
London Road
Kingston upon Thames
Surrey KT2 6SR
Telephone: 0181-547 3333

192 60067

While every care has been taken
in the writing and editing of this book,
readers should be aware that only Acts of Parliament
and Statutory Instruments have the force of law,
and that only the courts can authoritatively
interpret the law.

ISBN 1 85524 456 X

Printed by Whitstable Litho Ltd,
Whitstable, Kent.

CONTENTS

ABOUT THE AUTHOR

Robert Leach FCCA is a certified accountant who has specialised as an author on tax and financial subjects since 1984.

He is the author of 30 books and a contributor to 3 of Croner's newsletters.

INTRODUCTION

A stable economic basis and a coherent financial market have always been at the heart of the objectives of the European Union, and of the bodies from which the Union has developed. When it was first established, the then European Economic Community was more concerned with the ready provision of such basic materials as food and fuel in the aftermath of the Second World War. Financial services were a low priority. International financial dealings were in any case restricted by exchange control regulations set up to protect local economies. Although such controls were introduced as a wartime emergency regulation to protect the home currency and hinder the enemy currency, they lingered on in Europe into the 1980s. The UK was among the first states to abolish exchange controls in 1979.

Even today there is still no common European finance policy in the way that there is a common agricultural policy, although some elements of the financial market are affected by Europe as a by-product of other provisions. For example, the regulation of the accountancy profession is influenced by directives on mutual recognition of professional qualifications and on the free movement of workers. Pension provisions have also been considerably affected by European Court of Justice rulings on the issues of equal pay for women.

By far the most important financial development immediately facing Europe is the prospect of economic and monetary union culminating in a single currency. The single currency is timetabled to come into use for banking and non-cash transactions on 1 January 1999, and from then on to be phased in for other purposes. It is intended to replace national currencies from 1 January 2002 when there is to be a six-month transitional period of dual currencies. However, all the

1

grand ideas from Europe have come to be delayed. The single currency itself was originally intended to be implemented in 1997 but was delayed by two years and may yet be delayed again.

Economic and monetary union (EMU) has wide-ranging effects in all areas of finance. This remains the case whether the UK joins the first wave, a later wave, or even if the single currency does not happen at all. If the single currency does fail in its present form, the disciplines it has forced countries to adopt will continue. It is possible that a less ambitious revised plan might emerge from the ashes of failure. Many of the ramifications of such a development would be the same. At the time of writing, however, it is still unclear whether the final phase of EMU will happen because there is so much at stake politically.

This book starts with a thorough examination of the single currency, and in the following chapters explores how this one development will influence the various areas of financial services.

1. HISTORY AND THEORY OF THE EUROPEAN MONETARY SYSTEM

INTRODUCTION

The European Monetary System (EMS) is a fundamental part of the European Union's economic policy, committed to the ever closer union of Member States. The policies were developed during the 1970s when it was hoped that they would lead to a rapid convergence of national economies and the economy of a single currency.

All EU countries are members of the EMS, though their entry has sometimes been delayed for a few years after joining the political union, as it was for the UK. Strictly speaking, membership of the EMS is not a condition of joining the EU, nor is membership of EMS restricted to EU countries.

Originally the EMS comprised four elements:
- the Exchange Rate Mechanism (ERM)
- the European currency unit (ecu)
- the European Monetary Co-operation Fund (EMCF)
- the Very Short-Term Financing (VSTF) facility.

The ERM has been called the second stage of EMS, and the single currency the third stage. The EMCF is the means by which co-operation is ensured between the central banks of Member States. The VSTF is a means of financing the rapid assistance needed to keep national currencies within their ERM bands.

EXCHANGE RATE MECHANISM

The Exchange Rate Mechanism (ERM) started on 13 March 1979.

Originally this was intended to last just two years before the introduction of a more comprehensive system in 1981, but this never happened.

The operation of the ERM involved the creation of a new currency, the European currency unit or ecu, whose value is made up of a basket of national currencies of Member States whether or not they are in the Exchange Rate Mechanism. The UK stayed outside the ERM for over 11 years, finally joining on 8 October 1990 at a central rate of £1 = DM2.95. When the UK joined, the ecu was worth about 70p. Joining was initially warmly welcomed by the financial markets. The pound immediately soared to DM3.03, at one point reaching DM3.05. Since leaving the ERM in 1992, the ecu rate of sterling has varied between 83p in December 1995 and 70p in April 1997.

The German mark has remained by far the strongest ERM currency. From 1974 to 1995 the value of the ecu has fallen by 40% against the German currency, from DM3.08 to DM1.90.

The ERM originally had two bands, the narrow band in which currencies were allowed to fluctuate by ± 2.25% from a base value, and a wide band allowing for a ± 6% fluctuation. Originally only the Italian lira was in the wide band, though this was joined by the pound. National governments were expected to keep currencies within the band, and to start taking appropriate steps when a currency falls outside 75% of its spread. This trigger is known as the divergence indicator.

The Exchange Rate Mechanism faced a crisis within months of its formation in 1979 when the Danish currency was revalued, and France had a series of currency problems from 1981 to 1987. Yet the ERM faced these problems largely unscathed, prompting the belief that here at last was a system that really worked.

BLACK WEDNESDAY AND THE ERM

The UK and Italy were forced out of the Exchange Rate Mechanism on 16 September 1992, a day nicknamed "Black Wednesday". The sequence of events had started with a run on the pound and the lira. On 13 July 1992, the pound fell below the ERM rate of DM2.95 for the first time since the UK had joined. The problems were exacerbated by other economic factors, particularly the fast-weakening US dollar and building societies increasing their interest rates to compete with National Savings. On 5 September 1992, EU leaders categorically ruled out any realignment of currencies within the ERM. Eight days later the lira was realigned by a 7% devaluation — the second largest realignment in the history of the ERM.

On 16 September 1992, the pound started trading at 7am at DM2.7780, its ERM floor. The Bank of England and other central banks spent £10 billion trying to prop up sterling. In desperation, Chancellor Norman Lamont raised the base rate from 10% to 12% at 11am and then to 15% at 2.15pm before pulling out of ERM completely at 7.45pm — an action not actually allowed for in ERM rules. Interest rates returned to 12% at the same time (the only occasion that the base rate has changed three times in one day), and fell to 10% on 17 September 1992. In the next few days the pound fell to around DM2.50. Interest rates were down to 8% by 16 October 1992 and continued falling steadily.

Collapse of the ERM

The hiatus in the UK largely obscured British observation of the chaos elsewhere in Europe. The lira crashed through its floor just seven days after being devalued for the express purpose of preventing just such crash. Sweden raised its overnight marginal lending rate less 500%. The French referendum on the Maastricht Treaty was held four days later and achieved a marginal 'yes' vote.

On 2 August 1993 the ERM, as it then stood, in effect fell apart. The French franc was then trading at 5% below its ERM floor, forcing France to abandon its *franc fort* policy. Far from moving all currencies into the narrow ± 2.25% band, they were instead allowed to float within a ± 15% band, effectively meaning that EU currencies were allowed to float freely. At that time only 9 of the 12 currencies were in the ERM; the pound and lira had not rejoined, and the Greek drachma had never joined. The two founding fathers of the ERM (former French President d'Estaing and former German Chancellor Schmidt) pronounced the ERM dead.

With such a wide band operating, sterling could have rejoined the ERM. Indeed, had such a band been in place in 1992, sterling would never have been forced to leave. For UK Euro-sceptics there was further quiet satisfaction when the pound returned to its ERM mid-point value by June 1997. In the following month the pound exceeded DM3.00 — ultimately the markets had triumphed where the ERM had failed.

ERM 2

Despite the problems of the ERM, the European Commission has decided to introduce a revised version, known as ERM 2, as the mechanism by which non-participating Member States' currencies will be linked to the euro. This was agreed at the Madrid Summit in June 1996.

The main modification is that ERM 2 will have a "hub and spokes" structure where each "out" currency is pegged to the euro, rather than kept in a parity grid. It is proposed that "out" Member States may limit bilateral fluctuations between their currencies by bilateral agreements.

It is also proposed that there be wide fluctuation bands, though Member States may decide to move to a narrower band on an ad hoc basis.

Under ERM 2 there will be some automatic intervention at the margins, though with an escape clause to protect the euro's monetary policy. The European Central Bank (ECB) will be allowed to suspend intervention if its primary purpose of price stability of the euro is thereby threatened.

A realignment of currencies within ERM 2 could be initiated either by the relevant Member State (as now) or by the ECB (a new provision). The ECB would also have the right to initiate discussions on realignment if it believed that the currency values no longer reflected economic fundamentals.

It remains difficult to see how ERM 2 differs significantly from a system of freely floating currencies.

2. THE SINGLE CURRENCY

INTRODUCTION

The most significant financial development currently facing Europe is the proposed introduction of a single currency. Progress (or otherwise) towards the single currency is reported almost daily in the press, but most of this coverage is related to the political ramifications rather than the practical consequences.

In February 1997 the Commissioner responsible for the single currency, Yves-Thibault de Silguy, said that it would be introduced on 1 January 1999, as planned, and that participation would be beneficial for the UK. He also observed that preparations for the single currency were proving to be a good economic discipline for Member States.

The finance ministers' council (ECOFIN) met in May 1997 to review the convergence programmes of Member States. The plans for Spain and Portugal were regarded as credible, realistic and balanced. The Italian programme has been revised as part of the "new generation" of convergence programmes. The term "new generation" indicates that the convergence criteria may be manipulated ("fudged") as they cannot be met in their existing format.

In the spring of 1998, European Union finance ministers will meet to decide if the single currency should proceed and, if so, which countries qualify for inclusion. In reality, everyone expects this to be a decision on how far the criteria should be fudged to let those countries who want to join do so. Although only Luxembourg is likely to meet the criteria properly, the criteria can probably be fudged for any other countries except Greece. Germany, France, Belgium, the Netherlands and Italy want to join; the UK, Denmark and Sweden could probably easily do so but have indicated that they do not wish to be part of the first phase.

It has been argued that convergence criteria are not particularly crucial because, for example, a nation running a high deficit could simply "lean" on the creditworthiness of its fellow Member States. To prevent this practice, known as "freeloading", it is necessary for participating states to demonstrate a commitment to budgetary and political controls. The convergence criteria and stability pact are simply efforts to quantify these requirements. Such arguments will doubtless be used to justify Germany and France joining the single currency at its start.

If the single currency proceeds as planned, about 30% of the world's exports will be denominated in the euro.

WHAT IS THE SINGLE CURRENCY?

The proposed new currency is the third stage of economic and monetary union (EMU) as defined in Articles 109a to 109l of the Treaty of Rome as amended by the Maastricht Treaty. Called the euro, it will be divided into 100 cents and although the exact value has yet to be fixed, one euro is likely to be worth about 70p. It will become the common currency of all participating Member States and be an accepted foreign currency in other Member States and throughout the world.

It is intended that this currency be introduced for non-cash transactions from 1 January 1999, and for all purposes not later than 1 January 2002 (when coins and notes will be introduced). There would be a six-month transitional period to not later than 1 July 2002, after which all participating states' previous national currencies would cease to be legal tender.

Notes and Coins

Notes and coins have been designed for the new currency. There are seven notes (for 5, 10, 20, 50, 100, 200 and 500 euros) and eight coins (1, 2, 5, 10, 20 and 50 euro cents, and 1 and 2 euros) differing in size and colour according to denomination, but all containing security features.

The coins are all circular, a previous design of hexagonal coins having been abandoned. European coin designs will be applied to the reverse only; each country may individually design the obverse. It is assumed that any UK coins will incorporate an image of the monarch, as on current coins. However, coins bearing all designs will remain legal tender in all countries. If Greece becomes a participating state it will be allowed to issue coins with 'euro' and 'euro cent' in Greek characters.

The coins have been criticised by organisations representing the blind as not distinctive enough. The coins are thin by current standards and do not have the variations in thickness, weight, shape and milled edges that UK currency has.

It should also be appreciated that there are 70 billion coins circulating in EU Member States. It has been estimated that it will take all the European mints four years' continuous production to ensure that there are enough coins physically available, assuming that the mints had no other coins to produce. There are similar problems for bank notes, for which three years are required.

The Royal Mint is committed to issuing a new £2 coin from autumn 1997. If the UK joined the single currency, this coin would last less than five years.

Notation

The international symbol agreed for the euro is inspired by the Greek epsilon and the first letter of Europe. It is an 'E' crossed by two parallel lines, chosen to indicate the stability of the new currency.

The information technology industry is under pressure to prepare the necessary fonts, keyboard characteristics and codes for use in computer systems. The three letter code EUR will be used in financial markets.

Rounding

Agreement has been reached that conversion should be effected using the rate of euros to sterling and each other existing EMU currency only; no reciprocals should be used for conversion the other way. The conversion factor will be expressed to six decimal places, and the answer is then usually rounded to two decimal places. The rounding would follow the normal convention that the significant figures beyond the required places would be rounded up if more than 5, and rounded down if below 5; if the significant figure gives 5 as the last significant figure, the amount is rounded up.

This means that if, for example, the conversion factor is 1.352331, a conversion from euros to pounds must be made by dividing the euros by this number. So 4000 euros would be worth $4000 \div 1.352331 = £2957.85572$. This would be rounded up to £2957.86.

There are some occasions when rounding is required to more significant figures, such as when VAT is calculated on individual items. It is assumed that the normal arithmetical rules will also apply in such cases.

ADVANTAGES OF THE SINGLE CURRENCY

A single currency should make the economies of Europe perform as one. If one state fell behind, the other states would be pulled down with it. This is why participation in the single currency is subject to strict criteria and relies on the handing over of monetary management to pan-European institutions.

The advantages of a single currency are hotly contested between economists. Those in favour argue the following points.

1. The savings made by avoiding exchange rate losses could increase company profitability by up to 3%. This figure includes the costs incurred by business in hedging foreign currency dealings.

2. The European Commission has estimated that the single currency will lead to direct savings of 0.5% of Europe's combined gross domestic product (GDP). This is worth over £20 billion a year.

3. There would also be a boost to trade arising from savings such as companies having to provide just one price list and from price transparency between competitors in different states.

4. The loss of currency risk would be a boost to trade. The European Commission has estimated that this could further boost GDP by between 5% and 10%, though many see such estimates as wildly optimistic.

5. Individuals would save on currency exchanges. At present a traveller starting with £1000 and converting to the local currency in each Member State of the EU (but not spending anything) would return with £605, according to American Express.

6. A single financial market following from a single currency would also have the effect of constraining interest rate changes. This is an area where the UK is more vulnerable than other EU states, as about 80% of borrowing is based on variable interest rates. Put simply, the economic risk is borne by the borrower rather than the lender.

DISADVANTAGES OF THE SINGLE CURRENCY

The disadvantages of the single currency are considered by many of its opponents to revolve as much around the potential vast transitional costs of moving to a new currency as around the loss of political and economic control. Those who support the "stay out" campaign argue the following points.

1. The competitive gains from European integration will all be achieved in the single market anyway, without the extra burden of a single currency, whilst handing over control of monetary policy to Europe could be extremely costly and risky.

2. There are enormous costs involved in training staff, educating the public and physically producing the coins and notes, let alone the cost to companies who will have to modify corporate strategies, accounting software and pricing policies. It has been estimated that the costs of modifying coin-handling machines alone could amount to £11 million. EU retailers have estimated a bill of up to £30 billion, and the banks could incur costs of over £7 billion.

WHO WILL JOIN THE SINGLE CURRENCY?

Participation by a Member State depends on it meeting the convergence criteria and agreeing the stability pact. These are designed to impose financial disciplines on all Member States so that they perform at an approximately uniform level. In particular the stability pact is designed to ensure financial discipline for economic growth and job opportunities after the single currency has been adopted.

There are six convergence criteria, of which the two most important are:

-   national debt below 60% of GDP
-   annual government borrowing below 3% of GDP.

If a state meets the convergence criteria, the Maastricht Treaty requires the state to join the single currency. Only Denmark and the UK have negotiated "opt-outs" which give them the right to decide at the time whether to join.

At the time of writing, it seems that only Luxembourg will meet all six conditions. However, there is clear political determination that the single currency will start on time, even if it means fudging the conditions.

FEASIBILITY OF THE SINGLE CURRENCY

Even if the single currency gets off the ground, there is no guarantee that it will continue. Some critics point to the analogy of a cart which is hitched to horses running at different speeds — it will eventually overturn. However, some currencies have successfully stayed linked where either one economy dominates the other or the two economies perform almost identically. The Irish punt and the pound sterling were held in parity until 30 March 1979 with no apparent problem. The Belgian and Luxembourg francs maintain parity. The pound in the Falklands, Gibraltar and Channel Islands is at parity with the UK pound sterling.

Previous attempts at currency fixing have had limited success. The gold standard, for example, fixed exchange rates in terms of gold. This system was abandoned in 1972, but currencies were periodically revalued during its life.

In 1947 the International Monetary Fund (IMF) was formed, with one of its objectives being to stabilise exchange rates. In 1971, the Group of Ten leading members (also known as the Paris Club) agreed that currencies would not be fixed but allowed to float within a

± 2.25% margin of their new rates — this was later adopted as the narrow band of the Exchange Rate Mechanism. The dollar was revalued to gold at $38 an ounce, and most currencies were allowed to float freely in the latter part of 1971. In 1972, the pound floated again. Although described as a temporary adjustment, the pound never returned to fixed rates. By 1980, the system of floating exchange rates had gained general support.

NATIONAL CURRENCIES AFTER THE EURO

From 1 January 1999, participating national currencies will remain legal tender side by side with the euro and they will be regarded as denominations of the euro for legal purposes. There is no provision for a Member State to decide when a note or coin ceases to be legal tender other than, at the latest, 1 July 2002.

Under UK law, all notes and coins ever issued retain their value indefinitely. Demonetised coins will be exchanged for current coins only in multiples of £1, but old notes will be exchanged for current notes in any quantity. It remains to be seen if this applies after demonetisation for the single currency. In practice, most old notes and coins usually have more value as collectors' items. However, the value for collectors' items can depend on whether an item is legal tender or exchangeable for legal tender.

FOREIGN CURRENCIES AFTER THE EURO

For currencies outside the euro zone, the euro will simply be another foreign currency. There are many instances of smaller countries sharing the same currency, such as the CFA franc used by many former French colonies in Africa.

In April 1997, the European Commission produced a working document looking at the euro in a world context. Its main predictions are that:

- the euro could become an international currency being used by countries outside the euro zone in the same way that the US dollar is already used (it is expected that the US dollar, euro and yen will become the three international world currencies)
- the euro will not trigger any significant shifts in exchange rates
- Europe will become a much more significant player in the world economy
- international relations will be better balanced, with Europe playing a more significant role to counterbalance American and Japanese dominance
- companies in the euro zone will be less vulnerable to economic developments from outside (such as another oil crisis).

CONTINUITY OF CONTRACTS AFTER THE EURO

There has been considerable concern about the legal implications of contracts which span the adoption of the single currency. Although it is widely assumed that contracts will simply continue with any amounts redenominated, the wording of contracts does not guarantee that this will always be so. It is possible that some contracts may come to a premature end by the doctrine of frustration (which arises only under English law) or the invocation of a *force majeure* clause. Even contracts which include a reference to the ecu may have problems on the adoption of the single currency, as the definition of the ecu may not accord with the definition of the euro. In order to mitigate these concerns, all EU states have now passed legislation to ensure that the adoption of the euro cannot be used as a basis to avoid continuity of contracts.

In theory, the provision for contracts is covered by Article 109(l)4 of the Treaty of Rome as amended by the Maastricht Treaty. This Article reads as follows.

> At the starting date of the third stage [the single currency], the Council shall, acting with the unanimity of the Member States without a derogation, on a proposal from the Commission and after consulting the [European Central Bank], adopt the conversion rates at which their currencies shall be irrevocably fixed and at which irrevocably fixed rate the euro shall be substituted for these currencies, and the euro will become a currency in its own right. This measure shall by itself not modify the external value of the ecu. The Council shall, acting according to the same procedure, also take the other measures necessary for the rapid introduction of the euro as the single currency of those Member States.

However, Article 235 of the Maastricht Treaty will be used as the basis of regulations which will ensure legal continuity of contracts, and it is these regulations which have received parliamentary approval in EU states.

COMMERCIAL AND PUBLIC AWARENESS

It is recognised that any introduction of a single currency must be accompanied by a huge campaign of commercial and public awareness, not only in Europe but also across other continents. The European Commission is providing subsidies for awareness-raising and information projects on the euro, including seminars and workshops, newsletters and exhibitions. Such initiatives have so far come from a wide range of organisations including European federations of business and professional organisations, individual companies, chambers of commerce and banking organisations. Even school textbooks and children's play money needs to be expressed in the new currency so that three-year-old children do not learn a monetary system which is abandoned by the time they are eight years old.

The nearest equivalent situation experienced by the UK was the conversion to decimal currency on 13 February 1971. It is worth noting that four years before, the Decimal Currency Act established a Decimal Currency Board and stipulated the specifications of the coins. From 1969, coins were available to the public, including the 50p coin which went into general circulation that year. Charts and advertisements were prepared years in advance to assist the public understanding, but despite all these efforts and preparations, there was still widespread confusion.

It should be appreciated, however, that decimal currency did not affect the basic unit of currency, the pound. In fact it was only amounts below the old sixpence (2.5p) that did not convert exactly.

It is also worth noting that the government considered decimalising using ten shillings (50p) rather than the pound as the unit of currency. This argument was rejected on the grounds that abandoning the pound would be seen as a loss of faith in the currency and a *de facto* devaluation to a lower value unit. A government report at the time declared that it would "fly in the face of common sense". However, the euro is a lower value unit than the pound, and the move to a single currency is a far more radical change than that to decimal currency.

The European Commission considered public awareness at its meeting in Madrid in December 1995. As UK policy stipulates that it should be involved in all aspects of the development of the single currency, regardless of whether the UK ever joins, the UK has participated in these discussions. The view is that public awareness campaigns in the UK will only need to be run in earnest once euro notes and coins are in circulation.

According to the European Commission, the single currency finally gained a majority of public support in May 1997. Support has been growing month by month: it rose from 47% in April 1997 to 51% in May 1997. Its survey was conducted on a large representative population in all Member States, and also found that:

– 77% believe they are not well-informed about the single currency
– 67% want to know more about the European Union in general
– 82% want more aid to developing countries.

Information on the Commission's communications plan, *Euro: one currency for Europe*, can be obtained from: J P Malivoir, DGX European Commission, Brussels, Belgium. Tel: 00 32 2 295 37 87.

3. ACCOUNTANCY

INTRODUCTION

The UK has more qualified accountants than any other European country. Although European law regarding mutual recognition of professional qualifications allows accountants from one Member State to practise in other states, very few accountants actually do so. The differences in language, law and tax make an accountancy qualification gained in one Member State of little value abroad. For UK accountants there are far easier overseas markets in English-speaking former colonies, many of which have based their legal systems on the UK model.

It should be appreciated that UK accounting practices are far more subjective than those in other Member States. Continental Europe prefers the "cook book" approach whereby policies are detailed as thoroughly as principles. Thus a German company has no discretion about the time over which to depreciate a fixed asset — it has already been laid down.

Where it is necessary for accountancy to go beyond the limited scope of national bodies, international standards are more likely to apply than European ones. Such standards are slowly providing a measure of international objectivity and comparability into accounting.

Accounting requirements are themselves unlikely to be affected by the single currency and other European developments. However, there are likely to be more significant practical problems — many of which have tax implications — which need addressing as soon as possible.

The European accounting body (Fédération des Experts-Comptables

Européens — FEE) is building up a database of practical problems regarding the single currency. This information will be disseminated through its 34 member bodies to the accountancy profession in each Member State.

The lack of preparation by European accountants for the single currency was illustrated at the end of 1996 by a survey of large European companies conducted by the accounting firm KPMG. This found that four out of five had not estimated the cost of converting to the single currency on their business, and that only 8% had a budget to deal with the change-over.

In June 1997 the European Commission announced that it had drawn up guidelines to help companies to change over smoothly to the euro currency. Copies of the guidelines are available from the Commission at Unit DGXV.D3, C100 03/133, 200 rue de la Loi, B-1049 Brussels. Fax: 00 32 2 299 4745.

SINGLE CURRENCY CHANGES

Record Keeping

The change of currency raises certain practical matters in record keeping. It is assumed that most businesses will simply rule off their accounts at a certain date and then restate them in the single currency from the start of the next day — this is what happened when decimal currency was adopted in 1971.

The relevant provision is Article 7 of the amended Treaty of Rome, as follows.

For the purpose of complying with national legal provisions on the presentation and publication of accounts, the presentation in euro or in a national currency unit of assets and liabilities denominated in euro or in a national currency shall be achieved by arithmetical conversion at the conversion rates.

It is assumed that comparative figures for the previous year will also be translated into euros using the same conversion rates, though this is not explicitly stated in any regulation. There is no provision as to what rate to use for 5 year or 10 year comparisons.

One problem which has only recently been taken seriously is exactly when a company must denominate according to its accounting date. If its accounting date is, say, 1 April, and final accounts must be redenominated in 1999, this means that the company must start redenominating from 1 April 1998. As this date is now very close, preparations should be well under way.

Comparability

Accounts from companies in different countries would be produced in the same currency. Concern has been expressed that this could create a bogus comparability, as accounts of different Member States will be drawn up using different accounting conventions.

Rounding of share capital

If, as expected, companies round up their nominal value of share capital when they convert to the euro, many companies will see an increase in their share capital. This has implications for tax, earnings per share and dividend performance.

In UK accounting practice, rounding has rarely been regarded as a serious problem as the differences caused by rounding usually fall well below the threshold of materiality. However, this is not the case for rounding where the nominal value of shares is often a small amount, typically 25p. For example, if the pound is converted at a locked rate of £1 = 1.323901 euros, 25p converts to 0.330975 euros or 33.1 euro cents. If this figure must be rounded up to the nearest whole cent (ie 34 cents), the nominal share capital will have increased by nearly 3%. The dividend yield and earnings per share (eps) will correspondingly be reduced by about 3%.

Cost of Conversion

Another issue surrounds how companies will account for any costs of conversion to the euro. For an engineering company this may be the small cost of simple multiplication of numbers. For other companies, particularly retailers, there could be a huge cost involving printing new price tickets, adapting machines, reprogramming computers and training staff. There has yet to be any official pronouncement on how far such expenditure can be regarded as "extraordinary", but it is likely that it will have to be treated as an "ordinary" revenue expense. As extraordinary items are excluded from the determination of net profit for reporting purposes, this item in itself could make a significant difference to how a company is perceived as having performed.

Another aspect is separating the conversion cost from other costs. The obvious example of this concerns reprogramming computers. It is now recognised that many computer systems will crash in the year 2000 because they will either not recognise the last digits "00" as a valid data field or will regard them as signifying the year 1900. Many businesses face huge costs in making their computers "millennium compatible". However, if they do *not* address this issue, they will suffer greater expense when they return from their millennium parties in January 2000 and find their computers have crashed. Millennium readiness has nothing to do with the single currency, but as the two are happening at around the same time, many project managers have recognised the need to address both issues in their reprogramming projects.

Pricing Policy

It is not only the financial accountant who has problems arising from the single currency. The management accountant must also consider the implications.

A single currency will make products from different Member States more obviously comparable. This has many implications for pricing policy, and it may even mean that some manufacturers wish to change the size or other specification of their products. This phenomenon has become known as "pricing transparency". Suppliers will lose the ability to explain away price differences as being due to the exchange rate, and their problem is exacerbated by the free single market and greater mobility. It will be particularly interesting to see what happens to car prices, which at present vary widely from country to country.

4. BANKING

INTRODUCTION

The most significant event affecting banking will be the establishment of the European Central Bank (ECB). This will co-ordinate monetary policy to ensure that the value of the single currency is maintained. The euro is expected to take a greater share of non-EMU central banks' reserves than the existing currencies do at present.

As a separate development, the European Union is developing many rules for common criteria for the governance of European banks. One of the most significant of these is the Capital Adequacy Directive. The UK successfully fought a tough battle on this directive to ensure that its merchant banks would still be allowed to compete freely with the larger retail banks (which tend to provide the same services on the Continent). In particular, such banks are allowed a 10 day "window" in which they may trade in shares valued at more than 25% of their capital assets.

The various banking authorities are well advanced in their plans for coping with future developments, with alternative plans prepared for whether the UK joins the single currency or not. The British Bankers' Association (BBA) in particular has planned many initiatives to help its members prepare for the single currency. Individual banks are also well advanced in preparing guidelines.

However, the banking industry as a whole is going to be subject to huge challenges as a result of the single currency. These include:
- loss of foreign exchange trading income
- loss of cross-border money transmission income
- huge investment required on systems and products to remain in business

- the breakdown of barriers to entry for international banks into traditional domestic markets
- more disintermediation of the banks by borrowers and lenders.

The result is likely to be that many banks will be under great competitive pressure and many mergers are likely to occur.

THE EUROPEAN MONETARY INSTITUTE

The European Monetary Institute (EMI) is charged with providing the organisational and logistical framework for letting the European System of Central Banks (ESCB) function as one central bank with the European Central Bank (ECB) itself.

The primary objective of the central banks is to maintain price stability. At present, governments and central banks consider a raft of monetary indicators in deciding economic policy, principally rates of interest. The ECB will work towards developing a more common policy and implementing the monetary policy by steering short-term interest rates. Another aim with the method of achievement not yet agreed between the banks, is the control of monetary aggregates.

Although the policy will be decided by the ECB, almost all the monetary operations will be decentralised to the national central banks such as the Bank of England.

It is intended that the ESCB's main instrument of control will be open market operations, but national banks will also offer each other standing facilities. Open market operations will be undertaken at the initiative of the ECB. They will usually take the form of repos of eligible instruments and as tender operations with bids submitted to national central banks. These open market operations will be made regularly; it has been suggested that they be weekly with a two-week maturity, with parallel monthly operations with a three-month maturity, but the details have not been finalised.

There will be two standing facilities: lending and deposit. These may be used by counterpart national central banks at their own initiative. It is likely that the facilities provided will mature overnight. The rates charged and paid by the ECSB on the lending facility will be from the top and bottom respectively of a band within which market rates will move.

The ECSB Statute contains provisions for the possibility of reserve requirements. Work is being done to make sure this provision is ready for use, although most of the banking community, including the Bank of England, is arguing that the use of reserve requirements is not necessary.

Other instruments available to the ESCB include outright transactions, taking fixed-term deposits, issuing ESCB paper, and foreign exchange swaps.

It is a requirement that all ESCB operations must be collateralised. At present, national central banks have different requirements regarding the eligible paper they will accept in their operations. EMI does not expect to be able to harmonise these practices by the time the single currency is due to start. It is expected that there will be one set of high quality marketable paper for use at every central bank, but that some banks will also continue to accept high quality non-marketable paper from both the public and private sectors.

It is intended that open market operations and standing facilities will be available to many other bodies, known as 'counterparties'. These will include all credit institutions. For some operations, smaller groups of counterparties will be used. These will be particularly useful for fine-tuning operations which require short time-scales.

FOREIGN EXCHANGE AND RESERVES

The ECB may hold reserves of up to 50 billion euros (currently about £35 billion). This would be contributed by the national central banks in proportion to their share of the ECB capital. The final amount of reserves to be called up will be determined by the governing council of the ECB. This cannot be determined until it is at least known which countries will join the single currency. Only gold and non-EU currencies may be transferred. The currency mix is still to be determined.

The governing council will also determine the details of many other operational policies. These include:
- the organisation of foreign exchange intervention
- the handling of reserves
- exchange rate rules between the euro and the currencies of EU Member States outside the euro.

It is recognised that transactions in gold and currency reserves remaining with the treasuries and central banks of participating states could have implications for certain monetary aspects of the single currency. Guidelines are being developed which will require Member States within the single currency to give prior notice of transactions whose size or type could have such an impact.

For foreign exchange intervention, the ECB may intervene either directly or through national central banks. Various operational steps are being taken to facilitate this, such as a new telecommunications system.

PAYMENTS AND SETTLEMENTS UNDER THE SINGLE CURRENCY

The Bank of England has identified wholesale payment and settlement systems as the main area for which immediate work is required to accommodate a single currency. Much has already been done by the Association for Payment Clearing Services (APACS) and the Clearing House Automated Payment System (CHAPS).

Necessary changes to the existing sterling Real Time Gross Settlement (RTGS) system run by the CHAPS Company and the Bank of England have been identified. Under the CHAPS RTGS system, payment instructions are transmitted on a transaction-by-transaction basis directly between financial institutions. This transmission is made in real time, with full collateralisation of any intra-day central bank credit extended to participating banks. This arrangement prevents any intra-day settlement risk between members of the system which could arise in net settlement systems should a bank fail during the day and be unable to honour the payment messages it has already sent. In an RTGS system a transfer is final and cannot be dishonoured.

Other European countries are developing, or have already developed, their own versions of the RTGS systems so that they can also eliminate these risks. Technical arrangements are in hand to ensure that these RTGS systems can be linked between Member States via TARGET. These arrangements have highlighted some legal matters which are also being addressed, notably through the Settlement Finality Directive which is likely to be adopted early in 1998.

The UK's RTGS system handles many payments where the time of payment within the day is not critical. The primary advantage of the system is the removal of inter-bank risk (finality) rather than simply the speed of settlement.

TARGET

A pan-European system is being developed, known by the acronym TARGET (Trans-European Automated Real-time Gross-settlement

Express Transfer). The UK RTGS system will be linked to equivalent systems elsewhere in the EU, and will enable wholesale payments to be made in the euro, both within the UK and in cross-border settlements, whether or not the UK joins the single currency.

TARGET extends the risk-reducing benefits of RTGS systems across national borders. Central banks are tending to encourage its use, though its attractiveness will depend on its cost and efficiency and the extent to which customers value its speed and the advantage of preventing inter-bank intra-day settlement risk.

TARGET comprises one RTGS system in each country in the Economic and Monetary Union, connected by a network called Interlinking. However, other Member States may connect to TARGET. TARGET is seen as facilitating the operation of the European single market. For example, it will encourage arbitrage between financial centres, in turn allowing a closer linking of national euro money markets.

Work on TARGET is underway. The Interlinking project was completed in July 1997 to allow time for testing before monetary union.

The Bank of England intends to promote TARGET as widely as possible, and is pressing for its conditions to be made as attractive as possible. It believes this will maximise use and improve the overall security of cross-border transactions. However, it believes that any significant restrictions on TARGET which discriminate against non-EMU states are unlikely to lead to any significant reduction in euro activity in markets outside the euro area. It would simply mean the settlement of those activities would be made by other routes.

The cost of transfers using TARGET has yet to be established but, because TARGET must cover its costs, they are likely to be fairly high. To any TARGET transfer must be added the cost of using the domestic

RTGS system. Accordingly it is likely that alternative payment systems will still be used by corporations to effect same-day cross-border payments.

Ecu Clearing

The ECU Banking Association (EBA) already operates a clearing system for the ecu. In recent years this system has progressively been improved to attempt to meet the Lamfalussy standards on legal soundness, risk management and operational robustness. As a consequence the system now includes binding real-time limits. It also has the capacity for "circles processing", which may be able to unblock large payments temporarily delayed within the limits structure.

When the single currency starts, the EBA plans to switch to euro clearing. It will settle across accounts held with the European System of Central Banks and thus provide another means of making euro payments across borders.

The EBA believes it will be able to provide an attractive means of making less urgent wholesale payments, which should allow it to handle most corporate payments. With this in mind, the EBA is looking at ways of providing companies with information about its services.

Clearing House Automated Payment System

Clearing House Automated Payment System (CHAPS) is the UK's electronic high-value payment system, but it is also used for some retail payments. By 1997 the system processed a daily average of more than 50,000 payments, totalling some £150 billion.

CHAPS produced a report in March 1996 setting out a range of options for coping with the single currency, whether or not the UK joins. A detailed feasibility study regarding the euro has been undertaken. From this, CHAPS has decided that if the UK joins the single currency, the CHAPS system will become a euro system. The euro would be the designated currency during the transition period, with sterling permitted as a denomination of the euro. In addition, CHAPS will (from 1 January 1999) launch a new system known as "CHAPS euro". If the UK decides not to join the single currency, this will run in parallel to the sterling system, both in real time.

The link between TARGET and CHAPS will be via the Bank of England. Payments made to, or received from, other countries will be sent to, or from, the Bank of England.

The Bank of England will hold euro settlement accounts for CHAPS members. Euro payments will be settled between these accounts in real time. If the Bank provides any intra-day euro liquidity, it would do so by intra-day sale and repurchase agreements, as it already does for the sterling RTGS system. Liquidity provided against "repo"-ed securities would be subject to a margin to allow for market risk and any exchange rate risk. This, again, follows the sterling system for the RTGS.

If the UK joins the single currency, it is intended that the customers of CHAPS members will be able to send and receive payments in either sterling or euros during the transitional period. Settlement between CHAPS members and the Bank of England will be exclusively in the euro from 1 January 1999. Separate message fields would be used to carry the sterling denomination during the transition period.

Retail Payment Systems

The Association for Payment Clearing Services (APACS) has been working on developments for UK retail payment systems; it is assuming that the demand for such systems could be required from 1 January 1999, but may not be required at all.

APACS believes that if the UK decides not to join the single currency, there will be little demand for euro facilities for personal accounts, at least initially. It expects personal accounts to continue to be in sterling with the euro regarded more like a foreign currency. It is intended that this supposition be supported by some hard research organised by individual banks. There could be a demand for euro-denominated mortgages, for example, and possibly for other euro-denominated services. Even if the UK stays outside the single currency, it will need a euro-denominated facility to cope with such demands. If the UK does join the other monetary union countries, there will be a sudden and huge demand for euro handling facilities from the corporate sector. Details of the exact expected pace are being researched.

The retail sector has concluded that both the process of switching to another currency and the period of handling two currencies will result in significant extra costs. Representatives of the retail sector want the period of dual currency to be as short as possible.

Bankers' Automated Clearing System

Bankers' Automated Clearing System (BACS) is the widely used automated clearing house in the UK. It electronically processes credits and debits such as standing orders, direct debits, and dividend and salary payments. It operates on a three day cycle.

BACS is considering the technical options for medium to low-value payments in euros, and the desirability of these options vary according to whether the UK joins the single currency. At present it seems likely that BACS should be able to provide its service in euros for small business and retail customers. A task force has been set up by BACS to look at all these matters. One of its early conclusions is that there must be consistency and complementarity between BACS and the cheque and credit clearing systems in euros.

Cheques

Cheque clearing also operates on a three day cycle. The system of credit clearing processes paper credits on the same basis as for cheques. Cheques can already be made out in any currency, but any currency other than sterling is regarded as a foreign currency. The Bank of England has decided to leave it to individual banks to decide when to offer account facilities in euros.

The Cheque and Credit Clearing Company is investigating four options for handling sterling and euro payments if the UK joins the single currency, and whether a euro cheque facility is needed if the UK does not. The choice between the options will depend on expected demand, which is itself dependent on whether or not the UK joins EMU.

Debit and Credit Cards

At present in the UK there are several different card clearing systems with different procedures. The main two systems are VISA and Master-Card, which both process debit and credit cards through a central processor. Also important is SWITCH, which is a collective system of processing debit cards issued by various banks and building societies.

The APACS Card Payment Group is looking at the impact on payment by plastic cards. The problem area is in deciding when there is sufficient demand to justify providing a payment service in euros. The present thinking is that consumers are likely to want a euro card only when euro notes and coins become available. This will be 2002 at the latest.

Four years is considered adequate time to develop a euro card system. However, there will be problems if demand materialises earlier. The main problem is for the 500,000 retail "point of sale" machines, as these cannot generally handle two currencies. Some representatives of the retail sector have argued that such machines should continue to be expected to handle only one currency at a time. In effect, this would mean that there is no transitional period at all for electronic point-of-sale transactions.

In July 1997, the European Commission published recommendations proposing minimum standards for electronic payments. The paper covers transparency, responsibility and customer redress. It applies to payment cards, home and telephone banking and electronic money products (such as Mondex). These recommendations form part of an official communication designed to enhance consumer confidence in electronic payment forms. By doing so, the recommendations may make such payment forms more attractive and so facilitate the switch to the single currency. It is intended to seek voluntary compliance, but if this has not led to a satisfactory standard by the end of 1998 the European Commission will consider issuing a directive.

MONEY AND FOREIGN EXCHANGE MARKETS

The British Bankers' Association (BBA) has done much preparatory work on the impact of the single currency on the money market. The BBA believes that a euro-based London Inter-bank Offer Rate (LIBOR) will be required whether or not the UK joins the single currency. The LIBOR rate is used for settling cash transactions, over-the-counter derivative transactions and exchange-traded derivative transactions.

The BBA is also considering issues concerning the transitional period. If the UK joins the single currency, there may be a need for participating-currency LIBOR quotes during all or some of the transitional period. If the UK does not join, there will still be an eventual need for a euro LIBOR.

Practical matters being considered by the BBA are:

- the composition of various panels
- whether the new currency should be fixed on a spot or cash basis
- what market conventions should be used in accruing interest.

The last two conventions have now been recommended to the European Monetary Institute (EMI) by all international marker associations as:

- settlement on a spot basis
- day count basis for interest: actual/360.

The EMI's endorsement is expected imminently.

In foreign exchange markets, most participants are planning for a switch at the start of any transitional period.

SERVICES FOR SMALLER COMPANIES

In addition to the plans for banks to accommodate the single currency, the European Commission is also concerned about the quality of service provided by banks to small and medium-sized companies.

In September 1996 a Round Table of bankers and small and medium-sized companies was established. It established that most small and medium-sized companies were undercapitalised and want more from the banks than just competitively priced financial products. The banks recognised that their services to these companies could be improved. The report identifies several areas of good national practice regarding high-risk clients, risk assessment and private risk finance.

5. INVESTMENT

INTRODUCTION

The single market has long since completed the process, with few exceptions, by which investors may freely invest in companies in other Member States. Many investment provisions already treat the EU as if it were a single state, particularly in the rules regarding investment from outside the EU. The UK has been particularly successful in attracting inward investment from outside the EU, attracting about one third of the total. Future developments are therefore concentrated on the necessary adjustments to accommodate the single currency. As with other areas, the uncertainty surrounding whether the UK joins the single currency adds to the problems.

All financial markets have now reviewed the impact of the single currency. Some dollar-based exchanges have concluded that the single currency will have no impact on them. Other markets have started implementation work.

In Europe, there is a Federation of European Stock Exchanges which is looking at issues relating to the single market, single currency and other contemporary developments. The London Stock Exchange is represented in this Federation where it is a significant player.

In July 1997, the European Commission welcomed a report on the effect of the euro on capital markets. The report sets out the changes that should ensure that the euro-denominated securities markets are as broad, deep in liquidity and transparent as possible.

Non-discrimination

One of the essential features of the single market is that there must be no discrimination by a Member State against the competing products or services from other Member States. This can prove difficult to enforce for investments. For example, in February 1997, the European Commission referred Germany to the European Court of Justice for Treaty infringements because it was imposing restrictions on investment trusts established in other Member States.

Compensation

A new directive has been issued on compensation for investors. The measure requires Member States to ensure that at least 90% of an investor's claims are covered by a compensation fund when the investee is unable to make payment. Member States may set a ceiling of no less than 20,000 ecus. In the UK, such compensation arrangements are generally already provided.

SHARES AND SECURITIES

The adoption of a single currency will require nominal share values and share prices to be redenominated in a new currency. Member States agree on the need to do this by all of them adopting the same conventions. The opportunity may be used to harmonise other conventions as part of the same exercise, even though these are not directly affected by the single currency itself. The London markets have made submissions to the European Commission which is looking into these matters.

The London Stock Exchange is considering whether to have a "Big Bang" conversion of all securities to euros, or whether to allow companies to make their own decisions. It is likely that UK companies will be able to choose when to redenominate. It is also likely that UK companies may for a period issue some securities in euros while maintaining existing securities in sterling. The London Investment

Banking Association has expressed concern that allowing companies to decide when to redenominate could create a conflict between corporate freedom and market simplicity.

Co-ordination is also needed on settlement procedures. In particular, markets will need to be able to settle in local currencies and in euros during the transition period. There are four main areas of policy which need resolving.

1. Day counts used in calculating interest

Within Europe, the interest for a 31 day month is variously calculated as 31/365, 30/360 or 31/360 of the annual rate. It is likely that the convention will be actual/360 for money markets in euro, and actual/actual for bond markets.

2. The period between interest-rate fixing and settlement

There are variations from same-day settlement to a two day lag. For money markets it is proposed as spot, ie two days, and for bond markets it is likely to be T+3.

3. Price sources

Any conversion to euros means that the sources of security prices may disappear.

4. Timing differences

The differences regarding time zones and public holidays between Member States are expected to become more of a problem. The latest thinking is that settlements will be allowed when TARGET is open, which is likely to be every weekday of the year except Christmas Day and New Year's Day.

The London Stock Exchange introduced the Sequence programme in

August 1996. This contains a trading platform which can handle 36 currencies. Any new euro-denominated security can therefore be easily handled.

Although the existing systems can therefore easily trade securities in dual currencies, there are other problems in doing so. The Stock Exchange system handles dual currency securities by treating them as two securities. If there is a mass conversion of sterling-denominated securities to dual currency securities, there could be a detrimental effect on liquidity and significant additional costs arising from the near doubling of the number of tradeable securities. For this reason, the Stock Exchange is considering changing the existing system, even though it can handle the issue of dual currency securities.

There is also the issue of what to do about private investors who may wish to continue trading in sterling for euro-denominated securities. Investors may also wish to receive their dividends in sterling rather than euros. A common policy is being sought by the London Stock Exchange in consultation with practitioners.

As a separate exercise, the London Stock Exchange is discussing with the Department of Trade and Industry and other bodies how far existing company law and the **Financial Services Act 1986** can accommodate the necessary changes. The London Stock Exchange is also looking at its own rules. The preliminary thinking is that only minor changes will be needed, for example the current Stock Exchange listing rules allow only for sterling amounts.

The London Stock Exchange is also concerned that there is standard treatment across all markets. Whatever policies it finally adopts, it wants to see these also adopted by over-the-counter markets and by all members and their clients, as well as by other markets such as LIFFE.

Market Indices

The widely used FT-SE indices will continue after any introduction of the single currency, as will other indices for foreign securities, and there is likely to be the introduction of new pan-European indices.

In terms of coping with practical matters, there are fewer problems if the UK joins the single currency than if it does not. Even if some companies stayed in sterling, it is a simple matter to convert their share values into euros at the fixed conversion rate and to continue calculating the index much as before.

If the UK does not join the single currency there is a further complication of the additional element of currency risk affecting the index. At present there are few members of the FT-SE 100 index which trade other than in sterling. The most significant is Hong Kong and Shanghai Banking Corporation which is quoted in Hong Kong dollars.

The problem of currency risk on indices if the UK stays outside the single currency may be addressed by a new FT-SE index for euro-denominated securities. There are already FT-SE indices for foreign currency stocks.

CREST

Most UK shares and other securities are traded on the CREST system. This has looked at implications of the single currency.

It is expected that the wholesale market will quickly move to a system of euro quotes and settlement. However, dividends may continue to be paid in local currency for longer. This is not expected to be much of a problem on the retail market, as the retail investor will already have the facilities of sterling services.

No great problem is seen in the redenomination of share values in the CREST system; this matter can be fully addressed in a consideration of the legal issues involved.

The view is emerging that a security should only be quoted in one currency. CREST should not attempt to quote securities in both pounds and euros. The service of providing a link between sterling and euro investment for retail investors would have to be provided by the brokers.

In contrast, CREST would provide a facility for converting sterling inputs into amounts of euros. This would not be performed by the member. Some of the legal implications of this facility are being investigated.

If the UK decides not to join the single currency, CREST may still offer a euro-settlement option for equities and corporate debt quoted on exchanges in the euro area, though this is also subject to investigation of legal considerations. As CREST also provides settlement for Irish securities, it must also consider the implications if the Irish Republic joins the single currency.

Tradepoint

Tradepoint, established in 1995 as an alternative to the Stock Exchange, sees no great problem in dealing with the single currency. Its new systems are designed to deal with multiple currencies.

Unit Trusts

The Association of Unit Trusts and Investment Funds (AUTIF) has identified few problems regarding the single currency.

Most funds are denominated in sterling or US dollars, though it is possible to denominate new open-ended funds in other currencies. The Open-Ended Investment Company (OEIC) is itself a creation of the single financial market. It is basically a unit trust, but with much greater freedom as to where it invests its money.

One problem identified by AUTIF is the question of which tax regime will apply to euro-denominated funds, as it will become much more difficult to identify the country of issue.

Gilts

The Bank of England has established the Gilt-Edged Market Makers' Association (GEMMA) to look at the practical issues for the gilt market arising from the single currency. This body started its work in autumn 1996.

All Member States joining the single currency will issue new government bonds in euros from 1 January 1999.

Participating Member States must also decide when to convert their existing issues of government bonds into euros. At present there are too many varying factors to indicate likely decisions for each Member State, but a number have already indicated that they will also convert existing issues on 1 January 1999. If the UK joins the single currency at its start, there will be a law requiring all sterling gilts to be redenominated by early 1999. A particular problem is rounding, where even tiny differences after several decimal places can represent significant amounts.

The opinion of the Bank of England is that euro gilts would not pose any great problems for the financial markets, provided that the features did not differ too markedly from those of sterling gilts. The features on euro gilts are now becoming available.

All gilts will be issued in only one denomination. Redenominated gilts will retain their International Securities Identification Number (ISIN) to avoid confusion. The ISIN will represent the gilt in the currency in which it was originally issued rather than in the redenominated currency. It is appreciated that there could be confusion in having a security represented in one currency but actually traded in another; however this is considered the least confusing option.

The Central Gilts Office (CGO) will have the capacity to function in several currencies. This means that the system can settle stocks denominated in one currency against payment in another currency. It does not mean, however, that the system will be able to display two currencies for the same stock. To build this function into the system would be too expensive, as it would affect screen layouts and file-transfer records. It would also cease to have any useful function at the end of the transitional period, which may be as short as three years.

International Swaps and Derivatives

The International Swaps and Derivatives Association (ISDA) has established four working parties to look at the issues facing their work in a single financial market:
- legislation
- documentation
- tax and accounting
- market practice.

The International Primary Markets Association (IPMA) and London International Financial Futures and Options Exchange (LIFFE) are members of these working parties. A matter of great concern in this market is fluctuations in the rate of the euro. It has worked on the basis that the euro will fluctuate in a similar way to the existing ecu, and that contracts and market rules must accommodate this. The elimination of different conventions between markets could also be problematic.

Euroclear and Cedel

These two bodies provide settlement systems for bonds. Together they are known as the International Central Securities Depositories (ICSD).

Settlements in the ICSDs are automatically in the system for the European Settlements Office (ESO); the implications for them are the same regardless of which Member States eventually join the single currency. The work of these bodies depends on how the issuers deal with redenomination. Another factor is that redenomination is likely to create odd lots (ie blocks of security not in round numbers). Consideration is being given as to how far odd lots may be tradeable, and whether any provision is needed to prevent creation of odd lots.

Euroclear has concluded that most countries will adopt a "Big Bang" approach to the change to a single currency. However, Euroclear has decided not to adopt a "Big Bang" approach itself but to allow settlement in national currencies and the euro during the transitional periods. Users will be required to match settlement instructions in either the national currency or euro. There will be no currency converter built into the system. Euroclear has decided to leave issues of securities which mature before 2002 in national currency, which departs from other practices in the gilts market. It is estimated that about three-quarters of existing issues fall into this maturity period. For longer-denominated bonds, Euroclear expects issuers to use the nominal conversion arrangements to redenominate or exchange old bonds for new euro bonds, with a cash settlement of any difference. For cash management, Euroclear intends to use the principle of fungibility between national currencies and the euro — this means that Euroclear clients may hold cash balances in national currencies and in the euro, but that interest will only be calculated on the net amount.

Cedel Bank intends to retain nominal values expressed in local currencies but settle in the euro, but coupon, divided and redemption proceeds will be credited in the denomination in which the issuer has made the payment through the paying agents.

New government debt issues will be in euros once that state has joined the single currency. Member States have discretion as to when to redenominate existing debts during the transition period. It is expected that most will wish to redenominate early, though this could be affected by various economic and political factors. Because of the provisions of Article 235 of the amended Treaty of Rome, it is probable that all or most ecu securities in the ICSDs will be converted to the euro on a one-to-one basis, keeping their International Securities Identification Numbers regardless of whether or not the UK joins the single currency.

If the UK does not join the single currency, the ESO will remain the only system able to transfer euro-denominated securities, as the Central Gilts Office (CGO) would not have converted currencies. If the UK *does* join the single currency, the ESO will be one system able to transfer euro-denominated securities. However, there will still be differences between ESO and CGO in that:

- CGO will not issue gilts into Euroclear and Cedel
- gilts issued in CGO will be registered and dematerialised; gilts issued in ICSDs will be neither registered nor dematerialised.

It is possible that CGO may be altered to handle non-registered and non-dematerialised issues, though this is unlikely because of the considerable amount of work required to change the system. This work would also require a change in the relationship between the CGO and ICSDs. The upgrading of CGO software will follow the CREST system.

COMMODITIES AND DERIVATIVES

The single currency is likely to create fewer problems in the markets for commodities and derivatives than for shares and securities. Commodities are tangible items which can already be bought and sold in any currency, and derivatives tend to follow the conventions for the underlying security.

The London Clearing House (LCH) is considering the issues of the single currency for commodities and derivatives. It has already decided that the London International Financial Futures Exchange will include a converter facility so that participants may settle gilt futures in euros when quotation may be in sterling. It has also decided to offer euro cash accounts immediately when the single currency starts, regardless of which states join.

LIFFE is well advanced in its plans. By autumn 1996 it had amended its standard contracts for three-month interest futures so that they convert automatically to euros when the single currency starts for the state in whose currency the contract was originally denominated. LIFFE has also been listing contracts due to mature from 1999.

Variation margins will be denominated in local currency. LCH expects to enable settlement denominated in the euro or any local currency of a single currency state to be made in any other such currency denomination. Initial margin payments may be made in any currency. For these purposes, the euro will simply be just one more currency.

LIFFE's short-term interest rate (STIR) contracts will automatically convert to LIBOR-based euro interest rate settlement, when the single currency starts, if the currency is that of a participating Member State.

LIFFE has already established its provisions for STIR contracts in the case of day-count conventions for delivery months expiring in 1999. The principle is that the settlement rate will reflect the day-count convention of the underlying national currency deposit, even when the contract has been converted to euro settlement. For delivery months expiring in 1999, the contracts have interest rates determined on the basis of actual/365, except for Euromark and Eurolira where the basis is actual/360. These provisions are irrespective of the actual day-count conventions for the euro. By these means, the contracts prevent windfall gains or losses arising from the means by which the interest rate is quoted.

A decision on accepting securities denominated in euros for margin cover would be made independently of any decisions regarding cash payment. The LCH's intention is to accept such securities as soon as the cash market is adequately established. This is unlikely to be affected by other developments in the futures market.

LIFFE has been considering the most appropriate form of futures and options contracts for government bonds, bearing in mind that a euro bond will no longer reflect simply the economy of one state. Possibilities include introducing more than one type of euro bond future with separate deliverable "baskets" of bonds issued by each participating state. Another possibility is permissible groupings in a credit tier approach. The decision on the appropriate form is likely to be determined by how the market perceives the relative differences in credit risk between the issues. Whatever possibility is adopted, convergence of market conventions is essential.

Euromark Contract

LIFFE launched a one-month Euromark interest rate futures contract in November 1996. This was regarded as a development of the DM short-term interest rate products. LIFFE was influenced in this decision by increased activity in the DM LIBOR-based interest rate swaps and other contracts, as well as other factors. This new contract has shown a promising start.

LIFFE and Other Exchanges

LIFFE is taking the opportunity presented by the single currency to develop a network of strategic alliances with other exchanges in other time zones.

In 1996, LIFFE agreed such an alliance with the Chicago Mercantile Exchange (CME). This allows LIFFE's three-month Euromark future and option contracts to be traded in Chicago after the LIFFE market has closed. These contracts are the most liquid short-term interest rate futures in Europe.

It is intended that other contracts will be added to this arrangement.

Government Paper

If the UK does not join the single currency, it is assumed that the UK markets will continue to issue sterling-denominated government paper as at present. If the UK *does* join, it is assumed that all new paper will be euro-denominated from the start of the transition period.

The law is not clear on whether sterling-denominated paper may be redenominated. However, as most paper is of short maturity (ie less than one year) there is a view that there is no need to redenominate.

London Metal Exchange

The London Metal Exchange (LME) is considering how to deal the conversion of its 27-month DM and sterling contracts if either the UK or Germany joined the single currency in 1999.

The LME is also considering how to calculate forward rates for the euro against the US dollar.

51

International Petroleum Exchange

The International Petroleum Exchange is generally unaffected by the single currency as its contracts are almost wholly denominated in US dollars.

Baltic Exchange

The Baltic Exchange is largely unaffected by the single currency, as its contracts are denominated in US dollars.

Non-European Markets

The Bank of England is investigating how far the single currency will affect markets outside Europe. It is noted that European currencies have already risen as a share of private portfolios from 13% in 1981 to 37% in 1995.

THE 1997 PHENOMENON

Any consideration of the implications for financial markets of the impending single currency is confused by other more influential factors. In particular, 1997 has seen a rampaging bull market which started at the end of 1996. This has affected UK, European and world exchanges.

The general election in the UK has also had a significant influence. Traditionally, a Labour government is disliked by the markets, resulting in either a sharp fall after the election if the result is unexpected (as in 1945) or by heavy prior discounting before the election (as in 1974). On this occasion, however, the change to a Labour government seemed to be welcomed by the City.

In the first six months of 1997, the European stock markets have risen by 24% in real terms, according to the *Financial Times*. Opinions are sharply divided on whether this growth is sustainable, or if the balloon is just soaring for a spectacular fall. In New York there are already fears that the bull is out of control. Finance markets are largely governed by the herd instinct — dealers simply follow each other. Such markets also have the luxury and indulgence of self-fulfilling prophecies: because the gurus believe something will happen, the herd adopts a course of behaviour which is itself sufficient to make the prophecy happen, thus further enhancing the prophetic reputation of the gurus. There is also at least anecdotal evidence that anything which contributes to the "feel-good factor" boosts share prices. Thus the sunshine, short skirts, sporting victories and musical successes in the UK of spring 1997 have all been credited.

In yet another metaphor, the New York markets have been described as a students' drunken party for which there will be the inevitable hangover. Such arguments have credence when it is (occasionally) remembered that market indices are supposed to represent *something*. A stock market index is a mathematical representation of the value of the shares of listed companies. The share values reflect the underlying value of the companies, which comprises net assets plus goodwill. To the extent that share prices are represented by net asset revaluations, any share price increase is simply devaluation. However, the increase actually seen is in real terms, so it must reflect the goodwill element of the businesses. As goodwill is in effect the capitalisation of future profits, this can only be seen as optimism. As to whether this optimism is well-founded remains a matter of opinion on which only history can judge.

Dividend yields are very low, some below 3%. There is economic research to indicate that when dividend yields are below 5% a market crash is imminent. It is difficult to draw a parallel with 1987 as so many

53

circumstances are different. Dividend yields and p/e ratios in 1997 give a lower real value to the market than ten years ago; interest rates are also much lower now, making cash a less attractive alternative.

There are equally convincing arguments that these increases are sustainable. It is perhaps here that the single currency can become a significant factor. If monetary union is delayed, bond yields will rise and markets will fall. In turn this will make equities comparatively less attractive. If the single currency goes ahead, this should be good for the equity markets in states with weaker currencies (probably including the UK), as currency weakness makes exports more competitive and prompts further economic growth.

The 1997 waters are further muddied by other unprecedented phenomena. The huge amounts of windfalls paid by demutualising building societies have prompted a consumer boom and increased savings, both of which fuel market rises. The 1997 UK Budget changes regarding tax credits on dividends for pension funds have probably not had their full effect on company values, as the markets are still trying to work out what the long-term implications will be.

6. INSURANCE

INTRODUCTION

The insurance market is less affected by the single currency than most other financial sectors. However, the main considerations are:

- additional risks posed by the single currency and by conversion *to* the single currency
- how existing contracts may be continued into the new currency.

In general, the insurance market is confident that it can meet the requirements of the single currency with very little preparatory work, provided the banks are properly prepared. More work will be needed for the retail sector in such areas as notifying policyholders.

Lloyd's has long been a multi-currency operation. Its trust funds are held in US dollars, Canadian dollars and sterling; all other currencies are converted into one of these three. If the UK joins the single currency, the sterling account could become a euro account. If not, the euro could be converted into sterling.

There will need to be some work on amending the regulations and trust deeds, particularly in such areas as permissible assets. However, the solvency requirements would be little affected, as trust deeds already specify the relevant currency.

Lloyd's is to consider whether to quote in the euro if the UK does not join the single currency.

UNDERWRITING

The Institute of London Underwriters (ILU) already uses four currencies: the US dollar, the Canadian dollar, sterling and "convertible sterling". The last of these covers payments in all other currencies. If payments in euros become significant, the euro will become the fifth currency; until then, euro payments will be included as convertible sterling.

A greater problem occurs in parallel denominations, a problem peculiar to reinsurance contracts. Typically, such contracts are expressed in three currencies, with the exchange rate set at an artificial figure, such as £1 = $2. The problem is that the courts may not be able to enforce contracts specifying exchange rates which are not at such fixed rates.

INTERNATIONAL MARKETS

From 31 June 1994, the Third Life Directive allowed EU insurance companies to sell their products anywhere in the EU. Before that time, UK insurance companies were already deriving £6 billion worth of insurance business from other EU states. Annual premium income for UK life and pensions companies was worth £46 billion in 1994, which was 50% greater than for any other EU state. The UK was also the first EU country to have a formal compensation scheme to protect policy-holders against their insurer becoming insolvent.

EXPORT INSURANCE

The one form of insurance which is being most closely examined in Europe is insurance for exports. These are usually run or backed by the national government, such as the Export Credits Guarantee Department scheme in the UK.

The Amsterdam summit of European leaders in June 1997 resolved that state aid must be phased out as an element of export insurance for medium and long-term cover as it distorts competition. The national government should seek to withdraw from this area where the need can be met from commercial sources.

There is a proposal for the European Commission to issue a directive covering medium and long-term export insurance.

7. PENSIONS

INTRODUCTION

Pension provision varies widely across Europe. The UK has a private (ie non-government) pensions sector which dwarfs that of all the other Member States of the European Union put together. Because the UK now has such a large part of its pension provision in fully-funded schemes, it is much better placed than all other EU countries to pay for the high number of pensioners in the early 21st century as the "baby boomers" born in the immediate aftermath of the war reach retirement age. Other EU states rely heavily on government arrangements which are usually unfunded.

Around Europe

Pension provisions in other European countries may be briefly summarised as follows.

Belgium
Final salary schemes are offered by larger companies, typically using a rate of between 1.5% and 2% per year of pensionable service. There is a levy on employers' contributions to funds. Lump sum payments are taxed at a lower rate.

Denmark
Over half the workforce relies just on the low state pension. Private sector schemes are usually money purchase. There are few personal pensions. The tax system does not encourage private provision.

France
Most employees rely on the state pension and the mandatory pay-as-you-go schemes. Companies are increasingly setting up money purchase schemes.

Germany
Occupational schemes are common among larger employers, often with no employee contributions. The schemes are tightly regulated.

Greece
Little history of private sector schemes.

Irish Republic
Practice similar to UK, with most occupational schemes operating on a salary-related basis.

Italy
The generous state system has discouraged private provision. Some pension provisions are in effect covered by a system of termination indemnities payable when employment ends.

Luxembourg
Occupational schemes are seen as a top-up of the state scheme.

Netherlands
Industry-wide schemes are common. These vary widely in scope, but are usually mandatory for employees in that industry.

Portugal
Collective schemes are established only to meet the requirements of the strict laws. As an employee cannot be forced to retire at any age, some employers operate schemes to persuade employees to do so.

Spain
Salary-related schemes are becoming common as a means of meeting statutory obligations, encouraging employees to retire, and topping up the state pension.

It should be remembered that there are other relevant widespread differences in related matters. Retirement ages, for example, vary from 55 in Italy to 67 in Denmark.

Mobility

The European Union sets great store on the mobility of its citizen workers, yet EU pension laws, such as they are, prevent this in practice. Citizens may move to another country, but they cannot take their occupational pension with them.

In 1990, the European Commission set up a working party to compile a pensions directive. They established one and half of their three guiding principles:

- pension fund managers of one Member State may run a fund in another Member State
- pension funds may invest funds in other Member States
- a pension scheme may join a pension fund outside its own Member State.

The first of these principles was adopted; the second was adopted subject to a 20% limit; the third rule was dropped. The reasons were pure protectionism by Continental Europe: of the 256,000 migrant workers in the EU area in 1993, over half came from the UK and Ireland (Ireland had the majority with 77,000 workers, the UK 60,000). The provisions on equal treatment for migrant workers have been obstructed by tax provisions and legal obligations to join occupational pension schemes (now illegal in the UK).

There was also concern that the capital markets of the smaller Member States would suffer if all the pension funds could move to more attractive markets. There was a particular fear that Irish pension funds would all be invested in London.

THE SINGLE CURRENCY AND THE PENSION

A European Commission Green Paper on pensions published in June 1997 concluded that the single currency will help in the development of pension policies across Europe, though most of the problems will need other solutions. These problems are less acute in the UK because there is such a large fully-funded private sector for pensions.

The European Union favours supplementing state pensions by fully-funded schemes in the private sector — the policy the UK adopted in 1988. It does not favour increasing state pensions other than merely to index them. This policy of mere indexation has now been adopted by all the main political parties in the UK, though it was opposed when first introduced. In the EU as a whole, state-funded pensions still provide the bulk of pension income to pensioners.

The EU Green Paper looks at ways of maximising returns on pension investment income without compromising their integrity. Because of the cumulative effect of compounding over long periods, the Green Paper notes that even a small increase in return can have a significant impact on the level of pension provision. It is particularly concerned at the level of costs. UK private pension schemes can swallow up to a quarter of contributions in management costs in the early years.

The Green Paper also favours allowing pension funds greater diversity in choice of investments. This could improve liquidity and availability of capital. It is in this area that the EU believes the single currency will be of most help to funds.

Pension funds in the EU are already worth 1200 billion ecu. The European Commission is less willing to proclaim that about two-thirds of this is in the UK.

In 1997 both the Conservative and Labour Governments issued imaginative proposals for further development of private pensions. The Labour Government proposals, which are the ones that will now proceed, also envisage extending private pension cover to the low paid and those not in remunerative work (such as the housebound and carers). The former are likely to be effected by industry-based occupational schemes (more common in Europe) rather than employer-based occupational schemes. The latter are likely to be effected by contributions from the National Insurance fund.

The UK has almost single-handedly led Europe in the development of pension policy. Europe will benefit from the hard lessons learned in the UK, particularly in such areas as mis-sold private pensions, management charges, security of funds and any SERPS-type government scheme. The European Commission plans to produce a paper on EU-wide co-ordination of pension regulation.

8. DIRECT TAXATION

INTRODUCTION

Direct taxation is subject to a few provisions in the Treaty of Rome, whose main concerns are:

- free movement of capital between Member States
- free movement of employees and the self-employed between Member States, so there must be no element of double taxation or penal taxation
- no use of the taxation system to provide hidden subsidies for particular industries against their competitors from other Member States (the corollary of this is that no additional taxes or duties may be imposed on non-resident businesses or individuals from other Member States).

There is a general provision requiring a harmonisation of taxes, though little notice seems to have been taken of this in practice. In April 1997 a draft code of conduct was produced with a view to eliminating "harmful tax competition" between Member States.

The UK is, by European standards, a corporate tax haven with low rates and generous capital allowances. The reduction in corporation tax rates announced in the first Labour Budget of 1997 shows this policy is to be continued under the new Government.

EXCHANGE GAINS AND LOSSES AND THE SINGLE CURRENCY

The significant practical direct tax problem regarding Europe will come in adopting the single currency — that is, how any exchange gains and losses will be taxed on conversion. Foreign exchange gains and losses have proved to be a long-running intractable problem, only recently resolved in UK tax law.

No problems will arise after the point when a sterling amount is simply redenominated in euros at the fixed rate decreed at the time. It does, however, become a problem for certain continuing contracts, and even more so for derivative instruments.

The International Swaps and Derivatives Association (ISDA) has identified 23 types of derivative transaction, of which it believes 15 could give rise to tax problems. One example is a foreign exchange option between two currencies of states who have joined the single currency. It is not clear whether a taxable event would be triggered by the certainty of a net payment stream.

CRYSTALLISATION OF FIXED ASSETS

The European Union's insistence that exchange rates must be locked on 1 January 1999 means that companies will be forced to revalue long-term assets and liabilities expressed in foreign currencies. It is expected that this will crystallise values, leading to large tax liabilities. No satisfactory solution to this problem has yet been devised, and it is likely to be a particular problem in Germany. The pan-European accounting body FEE is looking into the matter.

9. THE EUROPEAN ECONOMY

INTRODUCTION

Although there is not yet a single financial market or a single European economy, for many years statistics have been prepared treating Europe as if it were a single entity. These statistics are a form of political "group accounts". In reality, the ratios and statistics are all averages of the Member States, so they provide the useful discipline of highlighting those countries whose performance is above or below average.

Like those responsible for national economies, the European Commission produces forecasts of what it expects to happen in the foreseeable future. Economic growth — the key statistic — was 1.6% in 1996, is expected to be 2.4% in 1997 and is forecast at 2.8% in 1998. Inflation is expected to remain around 2.2%. (The definition of "inflation" is measured by the new HICP index, as explained in the section below on statistics.) This figure is nearer 2.0% if Greece is excluded. It is the intention to bring inflation down to an average of 2.0%, including Greece.

Employment is seen as much more of an economic tool in Europe than in the UK. Total employment is expected to increase by 0.5% in 1997 and by a further 1% in 1998. EU predictions on employment have historically tended to be over-optimistic.

Across Europe, interest rates are converging at lower levels, exchange rate stability has improved, unemployment is reducing, and annual economic growth averaged 1.5% for the years 1991 to 1996.

BUDGET DEFICITS

All Member States except Greece, France and Italy are expected to have a public sector deficit for 1997 of 3% or less. This is one of the criteria for the single currency. The European Commission is pressing Member States to keep the deficit down by restraining expenditure. Public spending should be concentrated on investment (particularly in infrastructure), "human capital" and labour market reforms. This last item encourages other Member States to adopt flexible working practices which have largely been adopted in the UK.

As part of its 1997 Budget proposals, the European Commission has made recommendations under the excessive deficit procedure, which can result in suspension of payments. At present, Ireland, Denmark and Luxembourg have no excessive deficit. It is proposed that the Netherlands and Finland be added, and that recommendations be made to the other ten countries. The European Commission believes that those countries which have an excessive deficit and who have received funds from the EU Cohesion Fund — namely Greece, Portugal and Spain — have met their budgetary criteria for 1996 and that suspension of payments need not be considered.

BUDGET FRAUD

For many years, the EU Budget has been blighted with fraud, particularly large-scale fraud. The Budget now contains financial management proposals for the Amsterdam Treaty at improving measures to counter fraud. This includes new standards of propriety set by the European Court of Auditors and an inquiry by the European Parliament into the activities of organised gangs.

The European Commission has an anti-fraud unit called Uclaf which produces annual reports. One of its latest initiatives involves the development of anti-counterfeiting equipment.

In 1996 there were 4504 reported cases of fraud or other irregularity. These cost the European Union 1.3 billion ecu, about 1.6% of the annual budget. The figure for 1995 was 1.1 billion ecu, though the increase is generally believed to be due to better detection rather than a higher incidence of fraud.

COMMERCE

Commerce encompasses all stages from the supply of goods by the manufacturer through the wholesale, retail and distribution systems to the ultimate consumer. It does not include services, though it touches on some services related to trade in products.

Commerce accounts for one third of all EU companies, and 22 million jobs (about 16% of the workforce). Between 1982 and 1992, 2.3 million new jobs were created in commerce in the 15 Member States. This is a 12% increase, against a 7% increase for all employment sectors. Typically, commerce companies are small: 95% have fewer than ten employees.

The European Commission has identified four main challenges for commerce in the final years of the 1990s:
- the introduction of the single currency
- how best to use new information and technology
- differences in national legislation
- changes in consumer expectations.

There has been a marked concentration of larger companies, particularly in certain areas such as food. The European Commission believes that this is an area where competition laws need to be the strictest and where enforcement needs to be the toughest.

The European Commission notes that many commercial companies have extended their activities across borders, both into other Member States and into non-EU countries, and is committed to offering technical support to such companies.

As a separate development, the European Commission is looking at steps to harmonise national legislation affecting commerce.

COLLECTION OF STATISTICS

The European Monetary Institute (EMI) will prepare harmonised money and banking statistics for EU Member States. Certain figures are already prepared by Eurostat, particularly regarding balances of payments between Member States. It seems that Eurostat will continue, but share some of its competence with the EMI. The EMI is allowed to collect data directly from sources, but is expected in reality to delegate this to national governments.

Other statistics now produced by Eurostat will continue to be provided by them. These statistics are of prices, government finance and general economic indicators. Eurostat has undertaken to see how far national statistical methods may be harmonised. The main change so far is the Harmonised Index of Consumer Prices (HICP). With this significant exception, the current UK statistics produced by the Central Statistical Office and the Bank of England are broadly consistent with the European proposals.

In January 1996 the European Union introduced the HICP for the purposes of international comparison, and to ensure that Member States meet the inflation criterion under the Maastricht Treaty on a common basis. The index was set at 100 as the average for 1996.

Inflation measures over the last year only became possible from January 1997; international comparisons became possible from July 1997.

The rules for the HICP were published as Commission Regulations on 9 September 1996. The main differences between the HICP and the Retail Prices Index (RPI) used in the UK are as follows.

1. The scope of retail goods is different. The HICP includes personal computers, cars and air fares, all of which are not included in the RPI. Conversely, the RPI includes housing costs and council tax, not included in the HICP.

2. The HICP is calculated using the geometric mean, while the RPI uses an arithmetic mean.

3. Certain adjustments are made in the HICP to reflect changes in quality, in particular for cars and personal computers.

4. The whole population is included for the HICP, whereas the RPI excludes the top 4% and the bottom 4%, as their expenditure is regarded as unrepresentative.

The HICP is subject to revision with a view to the later broadening of its scope. It should be appreciated that the RPI remains the main measure of inflation. There is no intention to start using the HICP for calculating values of index-linked bonds, for example. For multinational comparisons outside the EU, a third measure is used: RPI less housing. This is used in the comparisons for the G7 countries (G8 if Russia is included). In the UK, RPI less housing is sometimes called "underlying inflation".

The EMI is required to aggregate national statistics and monetary aggregates from Member States. The UK methods are broadly compatible with these proposals. The EMI definition of a "bank" is wide enough to cover other types of financial institution in the UK, including building societies and mutual funds. However, many of the non-bank institutions will be excluded as being below the *de minimis* threshold.

One significant change in economic policy is the compilation of monthly balance of payments figures. This is common Continental policy, but it is not the UK practice.

STATE AID

State aid is generally prohibited under EU law, whether in the form of direct grant or tax subsidies. An annual average of £66.5 billion was spent by Member States in public assistance during the years 1992 to 1994. Most of this was spent on the manufacturing sector. In April 1997, the European Commission proposed stricter rules. The fifth EU survey on state aid found that the largest increase between 1990 and 1994 was one-off aid to individual manufacturing companies. This rose from 7% to 36% of overall volume, mainly because of the problem of addressing East German companies.

THIRD COUNTRY DISPUTES

The European Union is increasingly acting on behalf of all Member States in economic disputes with third countries. The European Commission is committed to a policy of open competitiveness where national economies are exposed to world market forces.

Common recurring problems are accusations of dumping (selling goods at low cost in quantity to destroy the home suppliers) from Pacific Rim countries, and the protectionist policies of the USA.

Examples in 1997 where the European Commission has acted on behalf of all Member States include:

- its opposition to the Helms-Burton law of the USA (this law sought to ban companies which traded with Cuba, and the European

Commission reported the matter to the World Trade Organisation for resolution)
- an agreement with Japan on reducing the difference in excise duties on imported spirits compared with Japanese spirits
- Japanese harbour practices which the European Commission regarded as an obstacle to trade
- Japanese regulations which seem unnecessary other than to deter non-Japanese countries from complying
- protectionist policies regarding the Indonesian car industry.

The European Commission also negotiates treaties on matters of particular concern with third countries. In April 1997, the EU signed a treaty with the Republic of Korea — the first of its kind — to facilitate trade and strengthen action against fraud.

Of perhaps greater significance are the mutual recognition agreements (MRAs) which the European Union concluded in 1997, separately, with the USA and with Canada. These are designed so that a European product which has already been tested for compliance with US or Canadian standards is not subject to identical tests in the USA or Canada. This will help speed up the introduction of new European products into North America, and is expected to be particularly beneficial for telecommunications equipment, medical devices and pharmaceuticals. It is estimated that the MRAs will save European businesses about $40 billion in selling to the USA, and $5 billion in selling to Canada.

EMPLOYMENT

It should be appreciated that in Europe, unlike the UK, employment is seen more as a fundamental human right than a private contractual arrangement. Also, employment is seen as something to be managed as part of the economy.

There are many provisions in European law on employment, particularly regarding freedom of movement between Member States and non-discrimination. The non-discrimination policy under European law tends to be tougher than under UK law.

The European Court of Justice has also decided that pensions come within the scope of pay, which caused problems when men and women had different retirement ages.

The particular European body charged with overseeing employment matters in the economy is the Employment and Labour Market Committee (ELC), which first met in February 1997. It has given a high priority to education and training.

INDEX

U

Uclaf 69
underwriting 55–6
Unit Trusts 44–5

V

VISA 36